'*Dropbear* is a breathtaking collection of poetry and short prose, which arrests key icons of mainstream Australian culture and turns them inside out, with malice aforethought. Araluen's brilliance sizzles when she goes on the attack against the kitsch and the cuddly: against Australia's fantasy of its own racial and environmental innocence.' **Judges' comments, The Stella Prize**

'This is a fierce debut from Evelyn Araluen. Her poetry, prose, and short-form non-fiction meticulously unravels the myth-making of modern Australia. This work is a powerful act of sovereign resistance, breaking open the intersections of power, race and colonial fantasy. In this beautifully written and carefully constructed collection, she writes from her own embodied Black experiences offering the reader a demonstration of the power of the Black writer.' **Judges' comments, Victorian Premier's Literary Awards**

'A deeply nuanced, sophisticated and self-aware book of poetry … *Dropbear* can teach us all if we are willing to learn how to read, to listen, to comprehend.' *The Sydney Morning Herald*

'In *Dropbear*, her debut collection of poetry, Evelyn Araluen wields a scalpel through twinkly visions and phantasma that treat the Australian landscape
The Guardian

'*Dropbear* is a living testimony to the power of words in the minds and hands of First Nations poets, activists and scholars as the works within this book speak beyond the surface to a deeper time and to bigger issues of unfinished business ... a work of agency and radicalism.' ***Sydney Review of Books***

'*Dropbear* ... simmers with rage for what has been done, but also glistens with a truly lovely softness when it reflects on land and family.' ***Good Weekend***

'While this is a book that works hard at dismantling the oppressive discourse and structures that dominate this country, it is also a collection that contains multitudes of love.' ***Meanjin***

'*Dropbear* is unapologetic and tough, dealing with issues of injustice such as Aboriginal deaths in custody and the ecological destruction of the climate crisis ... powerful.' ***Honi Soit***

'Funny, savage and really insightful.' **Annabel Crabb, *Chat 10 Looks 3***

'*Dropbear* pushes genre boundaries and, more importantly, brings a rich intertextuality of entanglement – the messiness of the relationship between us and the history of the country that we can't change and shouldn't ignore.' **Jeanine Leane, University of Melbourne**

'*Dropbear* is a remarkable work. The poems spark with energy and life. Araluen's is a dynamic voice that demands to be heard.' **Tony Birch**

'Evelyn Araluen dares to conjure old spectres, trope-busting her way through beloved Australian literary archetypes that still feed and sustain hallowed colonial fantasies and fixed-imaginings. This is an exquisite work of (un)reckoning and refusal where lessons and secrets reveal to unsettle and reclaim. A lasting imprint has been cast, storied with unnerving wit and wisdom and a heart so fierce and wide-open that we too love, pain, desire, and rupture through it all.' **Natalie Harkin, Flinders University**

'Evelyn Araluen's verse has an unrivalled and merciless clarity of expression and purpose. In *Dropbear*, she peers through her subjects, right into you – the reader. Evelyn drops her words over gazes and shoulders like a heavy blanket – obscuring or warming, it's up to you.' **Alison Whittaker, University of Technology, Sydney**

'In this collection, Evelyn Araluen lovingly honours ancestors and country, while she relearns the Aboriginal languages of place and home. At the same time, she ardently critiques settler colonialism, Australiana kitsch, and empty acknowledgements. Throughout, her voice rises and falls like the landscape, her sentences carve the page like rivers, and her words burn a pattern across time like fire. "These are the dreamings we have now," she tells us. Listen closely, reader. "Listen to the end."' **Craig Santos Perez, University of Hawai'i, Mānoa**

'Evelyn Araluen, right out of the gate with her first book, has shown herself to be a writer of formidable power and grace. You'll never see Snugglepot and Cuddlepie in the same way again. This is an electrifying debut.' **Michael Williams**

'The rigorous studies of language and colonial inheritance and political refusal in this collection are infused with a grace and ambition that wowed me. *Dropbear* acts as a testament of what has happened and what is yet to come. An important debut!' **Billy-Ray Belcourt, University of British Columbia**

'A book-work of incredible depth and complexity ... *Dropbear* can teach us all if we are willing to learn how to read, to listen, to comprehend.' **John Kinsella**

'Makes me feel, variously: awed, amused, tickled, confronted, told, envious. So, so smart.' **Kaz Cooke**

Evelyn Araluen is a poet, researcher and co-editor of *Overland* literary journal. Her widely published criticism, fiction and poetry have been awarded the Nakata Brophy Prize for Young Indigenous Writers, the Judith Wright Poetry Prize, a Wheeler Centre Next Chapter Fellowship, and a Neilma Sidney Literary Travel Fund grant. Born and raised on Dharug Country, she is a descendant of the Bundjalung Nation.

DROP BEAR

EVELYN ARALUEN

UQP

First published 2021 by University of Queensland Press
PO Box 6042, St Lucia, Queensland 4067 Australia
Reprinted 2021 (five times), 2022 (four times), 2023

University of Queensland Press (UQP) acknowledges the Traditional Owners
and their custodianship of the lands on which UQP operates. We pay our respects
to their Ancestors and their descendants, who continue cultural and spiritual
connections to Country. We recognise their valuable contributions to Australian
and global society.

uqp.com.au
reception@uqp.com.au

Cover design by Jenna Lee
Author photograph by Stuart Spence
Typeset in 11.5/14 pt Adobe Garamond by Post Pre-press Group, Brisbane
Printed in Australia by McPherson's Printing Group

 **Queensland
Government** This project is supported by the Queensland
Government through Arts Queensland.

  University of Queensland Press is assisted
by the Australian Government through
the Australia Council, its arts funding and
advisory body.

A catalogue record for this book is available from the National Library of Australia.

ISBN 978 0 7022 6318 7 (pbk)
ISBN 978 0 7022 6492 4 (epdf)
ISBN 978 0 7022 6760 4 (epub)

University of Queensland Press uses papers that are natural, renewable and
recyclable products made from wood grown in well-managed forests and other
controlled sources. The logging and manufacturing processes conform to the
environmental regulations of the country of origin.

To Mum and Dad, it's an honour to honour you.

*For J, every word. Before or after, and no matter
what survives us, be it horizons, highways, poems or stars.
Every word, and every place it came from.*

CONTENTS

DEBRIS

GATHER

GATHER

always to
    all ways

      slipping round the   every /

          light split   to share

          the leaf
          the branch
of skin /

sky open
    wide morning

            moves
            long gaze /

     it gathers   and it wanders
   at bare arms /

             it
          spills,   and
          me /

gather   bury   dry   burn
                 bread   cloth /

the word for bead   the word for cloth /

                              I gather branch /

                                   stretch of weed
                                   through creek /
                                   weave of reed /
                                      cord of

                                   throat that hums /

gathered story to you, girl /

    got something for you to swallow

The Ghost Gum Sequence

There's ghosts in the reserve. There's a rusted windmill and water tank, old concrete feeding troughs and burnt-out cars that crawl with the living – goannas, stray dogs, panthers. Every life I have knows this reserve and the liminal scrub it spills through the suburbs, which swallows the correctional complex to the west and edges up to the cattle station on the east. I can tell you how to find them, standing stark between a broken fence and a recurring dream of mama roo bounding broken away from the hood of my neighbour's car. Take forty steps back from where she fell and follow the creek that makes its bed now only in reeds and memory. Go at the golden hour when the sun slants sideways and watch their skins soak the light, or pass by on a cold early morning and see them soft blue silking through scratches of tall grass and bush pea. Watch below for blue-tongues and red-bellies, watch above for black kites and golden orb weavers. I'm not worried about you finding all this, I'm worried about how you're gonna speak it.

I've gotta go to town now, but I'll be back tomorrow. There's woven reeds and feathers on the dash, and I only clean out the dirt when I have to. It's about $20 to go north and $10 south, but it'll only cost you the petrol to cut through the cheap seats, the browning outskirts and housing estates where all my Elders live. I take Richmond Road slower in the dry, when everything comes out for the green. I've seen South Creek swell this plain they're cutting up for lines of neat houses all along this way, but they'll never come for the scrub. They need this scrub to keep the ghosts in. They'll come for the poor, longway streets first, and close off every path to leave without paying. All these roads meet and end and begin at the open field that once always-was-always-will-be was the Native Institution where Governor Macquarie gathered up the precious children, black and brindle, to teach them God and Civilisation and To Be Without Your Family Or Your Land Or Your Name. It was here that Maria, daughter of Yellomundee son of Gombeeree leader of the Boorooberongal, the place I go monthly to cut lantana and take my shoes off at the feet of ancestors, was taught white man's language, and how to scream it back to him.

Why don't they build something there? a sunset profile picture asks on the community Facebook group where grumpy home owners gather to buy and sell and complain. *There's nothing in that field but a tree.*

There's a lot to say about that and even more to say of this place, but today I'm taking the mid-range toll to the city, so I slip round the road trains and keep driving. I've been lugging a childhood from Dad's shed to Sydney in the boot of my car and it's getting restless. The little gumnuts are creeping from the pages to play patty cake with the yuri men on my back seat, tucking themselves under discarded jackets and licking droplets from the blackorg-branded water bottles collecting under my seat. They want me to write about them – or maybe they don't, and they just want to be left where and when they are – but, in any case, they're enjoying the ride. With their little faces pressed to the window, they watch tree turn to town, and hiss and shudder as we pass the earthmovers stacked at the post-Maccas merge. I don't take new ways to go to places I've known already, and I'm not likely to ever turn early from the M4, but there's something about those green-signed end destinations that reminds me of everywhere else I'm supposed to be. Sometimes I think I could keep on south, trace the banksia tattoos of all my Boorooberongal girls kicking about in Naarm, and then wrap them all up and bring them home. Sometimes I see the Canberra turn-off and remember it's been almost two years since I last made tea and stood in the eternal smoke of the embassy. But mostly I think, I know I've never taken that way to go to Nan's, but maybe if I had a little more often there'd be more memories to choose from when her absence moves my mind from room to room.

There's a lot of poets over in the mountains, or further up the Hawkesbury on the way to Nan's farm, but it was written for me to be born in this land and to die in this land long before I became a poet myself. The Cumberland Plains of Blacktown and the Hawkesbury are drenched in a history of settler violence and forgetting that goes unspoken when we squabble over heritage. The bridge, the dairy, the statue – competing heirlooms for the pastoral squattocracy now crowded by mid-density suburban sprawl. When Watkin Tench stood at Prospect Hill in 1789, he soliloquised Miltonic visions of this place he looked upon as a wild abyss. Shortly after, the rich alluvial soils were carved up by fence and crop and hoof and were cartographied into the names of holy lands: Jericho, Mamre, Ebenezer. Here was to be known as the breadbasket of the colony. A magic pudding for the settlers to eat, and eat, and eat. Somewhere in all this tabula rasa and terra nullius my black and convict ancestors met, each from somewhere else between one and two centuries – some taken, some lost, some left. We try to care through entanglement. We know where and why of the summer solstice. We know how to swim against spirits and contamination. We know where we will come back.

I look over to Prospect Hill as I pass through the M4 roadworks. In the way I know all times are capable of being, Tench's gaze is still there – but so is ours, staring back.

Learning Bundjalung on Tharawal

Above his desk it is written:
I wish I knew the names of all the birds

I know this room through tessellation of leaf and branch,
wurahŋ-bil and jaran-gir,
in the shade of a kulsetsi –
(Cherokee) 'honey locust' [a flowering tree]

I am relearning these hills and saltwaters
and all the places wrapped around this room
we both have dagahral here,
lovers/fathers/friends/conquerors/
ghosts

But here, in this new and ancient place,
I ask him to name the song that swoops through this mosaic:
sometimes it is wattlebird sometimes it is currawong –
when we drive, he tells me king parrot, fairy wren, black cockatoo

and I know jalwahn and bilin bilin and ngarehr
but the rest are just nunganybil,
the rest are just: 'bird'

It is hard to unlearn a language:
to unspeak the empire,
to teach my voice to rise and fall like landscape,
a topographic intonation

So in this place the shape of my place
I am trying to sing like hill and saltwater,
to use old words from old country I am so far from:
      bundjalung jagum ngai, nganduwal nyuyaya,
and god, I don't even know
          if I'm saying it right

But I watch the bark twist:
grey and slate and vanilla and vermilion
      he tells me this is ribbon gum –
so I find five words for this bark
and I promise I will learn them all

        Because to hold him is to hold the tree
          that holds these birds I cannot name,
            and a word spoken here
              might almost sound like home

We are relearning this place through poetry:
      I open my book and say, wayan,
here is a word which means road, but also root
and in it I am rooted, earthed,
singing between two lands
      I learn that balun is both river and milky way,
      and that he is baray-gir, the youngest child
      and the top of the tree,
      where the gahr will come to rest –
      to call its own name
      across the canopy,
      long after his word for it
      is gone.

SUBURB PARATEXT

lately i've been footnoting social space with con and para text, corner lingering too far from home under late-night unlocal neons // i dress in translation to arrive late at the party and sit at the back of the function, on the furthest edge lounge, drinking my own others with bottom fridge piss: [raising found vessel to fields swung violet sixteen] // it comes out a dollar a standard unless you've remembered that one simple trick to make your belly small, then it's like your liver is a voucher for four cents free a litre that you leave on the dash for the durrie run, for all that a servo is good for in this town // lately i've been playing battleships with the six drinks deeper, unfolding time immemorial against six generations settled six figures earned six continents conquered, an encounter mathematically certain for even such an eastsub twentysomething life lived but a first, a second, perhaps // amidst opinion and permission a backlit focus group surveys my influence on the revolution inscribed on shirts i don't wear in these suburbs // fuck suburbs without servos, and *from beneath i am above all this*, says this scene's comment section // these nights are held-tongue cemeteries of unread article tabs, they aren't the time or place but they're full of the wined ones on which i waste all my learned words for this place, the ones for whom i give sandstone stories and voice edge and twitter trials // such nights forget that every field i ever stumbled through was stolen, forget sixteen violent in handmedown dreams of dresses i'd never threadbare, of belly fuller than any of my generations before // such nights forget the choice in nights, a channel a switch, the drive west tolled to an occupying state, a screen dark on setting: a home //

Bastards from the Bar

       Whose revolution was it anyway
       that they peeled off a table outback.
The King George, the Hero of Waterloo, the ten shillings to
keep off the cops and a pack of durries in your shirt might
make it til morning from the long-haired comrades talking
jaundiced shit at the bar. They remember the verse and not
the bloody teeth, that tired songbird myth, the fucked-up
Sydney grammar dendrology. You remember
to retell me of a generation dragging themselves up the
frozen gutters of the cross thirsting for a fix, hearing
them spit guts and call it a page, singing broken bars like
harpooned ghosts. There will always be ash in your throat,
and you say you'll never miss the sixties or Sussex St.
I learn hate and love and men from the sound of your voice
spinning out the intergenerationality of wars too close for
forgiveness. Nothing makes violence holy, resolves the prize,
gives room in harm for legacy. I know the poem and it lied:
it never once stepped from city to bush, never climbed from
the drain or fought for more than a loose line. The poem
doesn't admit they forgot politics after the vote, and the
forest lodge can't tell us the world had changed, just pour
more out for the spectres waiting at the public bar. For what
they did to the women, and what they never did for us, it's
worth growing older, leave them fumbling for demons in
       broken glass.

Index Australis

Straya is a wild straggly abyss
with one fence struck through
a line of tin dogs guarding the coal from the flies
Straya is brown and sharp
when you watch it through the car window
through the convex humming screen

Straya in sepia 35 mm with sweat rolling across a tan
with that thin shirt sticking to skin
Straya trailing tin foil through red dirt
on its way to the pool party in the inland sea
the doof in the desert the biggest baddest bash
since time immemorial
everyone wants to rave in the oldest earth on earth

No law against that, no laws for nothing
in the age of entitlement
in the Decolonial Dundee
and well may we say, we will decide
who and how
well may we be not lectured and well
may we do it slowly

But darl, this is a drama not a document
Straya is a man's country
and you're here to die lovely against the rock
to fold linenly into horizon
and sweat beautiful blonde on the beach

Baby, don't you know this is a weeping song
and you'd be so beautiful in that brown creek

PYRO

THE SOLAR PANELS THAT SUNK US INTO DEBT
HAVE OVERHEATED SO THIS GASPING AIR
PRESSES WINDOWS AND DRAGS BODIES TO
THE FLOOR // LAST WEEK WE HAD TO FELL THE
IRONBARK THAT HAS HELD KOOKABURRAS IN
WATCH ABOVE US LEST THEIR FEATHERS CATCH
LIGHT FROM THE FLAMING LEAVES THAT FALL
FROM THE AIR // INSTAGRAM PROMOTES A SNEAK
PEEK PRE-COLLECTION OF ORGANIC COTTON
WOMENSWEAR IN WHICH THE THIN WHITE
MODEL LEANS DOUR AGAINST A FIRE TRUCK
IN THE THRICE-BURNT CHAR OF A HOMELAND
// I STAND PRICKLE RASHED LEARNING HOW
BROWN MY SKIN CAN BAKE AND BEG MY DOG
WHO AT THREE MONTHS OF LIVING IS YET TO
KNOW RAIN TO STOP STRAINING AT THE LEAD
AND JUST PISS ON THIS HOT HARD EARTH // I
READ IT WILL TAKE TEN YEARS FOR FLOWERING
TREES TO AGAIN SUSTAIN WORKING BEES //
FOR THE ALLOCASUARINA TO GROW SEED
FOR THE GLOSSY BLACK COCKATOO // MY
MOTHER CRIES QUIETLY AND YOKES WET RAGS
ACROSS HER NECK // MY FATHER COLLECTS
DRY BRANCHES WHEN ARRANGING THE YARD
INTO GRADATIONS OF THAT WHICH WE ARE
MOST WILLING TO LOSE // MY SISTERGIRL'S
PHONE IS TOO HOT FOR HER TO HOLD TO
HER FACE WHEN I CALL TO ASK HOW MANY
MATTRESSES HER FAMILY NEEDS // A GIRL IN

AMERICA POSTS LINKS TO PURCHASE HER
UPCOMING CLI-FI NOVEL UNDER HEADLINES
FOR THE PYROCUMULUS // SCOTT MORRISON
SITS SANGUINE IN A WREATH OF FRANGIPANI
// A VIDEO ON TWITTER PLAYS THE HOWLS OF
A BILLION RELATIONS ALIGHT // AGAIN WE ARE
UNHEARD AS WE SPEAK KNOWINGS WE HAVE
CARRIED TO CARE FOR THIS PLACE THROUGH
RECKONING // AGAIN AGAIN WE ARE TOLD TO
BE GRATEFUL FOR THIS GIFT AS IF THE MACHINE
HAS FIREPROOFED ANYTHING BUT ITSELF // I
WROTE THIS POEM AT A DESK COVERED IN ASH

Malay

malay cracks the morning
and prises suburban from the scrub
the first time I've heard her in this hazy place
where lawns edge bush brushes
and tyres swing from goanna trees
where blue-eyed babes won't
walk beyond the fence line
cos those dodge city boys
might be looking for a feed

she don't follow me through town
when I speak her that way
this cobblestone mountain shadow town
rivering up settlement grants
and decaying into city spread

Dad's not worried
like those other honeyeaters
got him worried
reckons they're here to push out the rest
to soak up all the green sprouting
from that last big burn
        that one
        when he refused
        to leave

swear it wasn't like this before
never heard that snap or bell drop
never had to pay for the M4

never saw nothing but tree on that horizon
a scene of semirural whinge

went back the other day
        to dodge city
council must have fixed up the dam
but it's still that same dust
those same boys bumming smokes
bruising bellies on crumbling bike mounds
crashlining crucifixes from londonderry to llandilo

after I could go to woollies
after I could swing by costco
after I could see a doctor or catch a train to town
get that city commute down to fortyfive by twentytwenty
drag the city to dodge
        and bring back maccas on the way

I drive to castlereagh to remember my horizons
maybe wear my feathers to remember emu scrub
I leave the path in yellomundee
        become skin amongst skins
        that have no other memory of this place

just before dusk
I collect two minutes and thirty seconds
of an old gahr-filled gum on my phone
to hear again and again
as their white wings slip gold in sinking sun
as their cries rattle still enough sky

I show Dad
as he washes up after tea
we watch as we are mountain watched
        remember this call
        remember enough

Playing in the Pastoral

The ~~evocation~~ entanglement ~~entrapment~~ of ~~convictions~~
complexes ~~consequences~~ which have, since **invasion**, ~~haunted~~
structured ~~hallowed~~ **settler** responses to, and representations
~~restraints~~ of **Aboriginal land** ~~home~~ and its **custodians**,
ruptures at its most ~~revolting~~ readable in Australian poetics.

> (Here are the adventures of the bush bandits,
> the buds and flowers, the babes and boys.)

Thru McLaren thru Indyk thru Griffiths thru Kane thru Taylor:
     The putative telos of the national character arising from
a shared ~~stolen~~ experience of 'the hostility of the landscape to
man's efforts to tame it' moves anxious ~~as if wounded while~~
~~wounding~~ around ~~over~~ **Aboriginal land and its custodians** in
~~fearful~~ cosmic, ~~suspicious~~ embodied, and negated ~~voids~~ forms.
In this configuration, the <u>People</u> and <u>Place</u> are *artifactualitied* to
~~remember~~ register in alternately hostile and picturesque images
of design/desire.

> and it was dreamt: the country where men might
> live in a sort of harmless Eden
> but it was: rather like falling out of a picture and
> finding oneself on the floor, with all the gods
> and men left behind

The reckoning [of the pastoral not as genre but as a series of
modes which assimilate natural and human worlds into objects
of white Endeavour] has been mobilised for a range of ~~social~~
national ~~socialist~~ concerns.

For: the well-meant impetuosity of a young colony.
For: the space and sun and unworn-out air.
For: the settler move to innocence.
For: the vacant office in the *Bulletin* for some
mythological creature to make itself useful.
For: the storm blowing from paradise.

These concerns have produced a ~~bargain bin of quilting fabric~~
complex and at times contradictory ~~assault~~ aesthetic of <u>kitsch</u>,
and the broader structure of ~~afternoon cartoons and childhood
bookshelves~~ <u>Australiana</u> through which it operates.

Dropbear Poetics

       Tiddalik say
I'm such great thirst
I will drain the land
and drag my big fat belly
across the empty sea

       Bunyip say
I'm gonna gobble you up
if you step waters where I sleep
and with wet claws I will snatch
your spine and ankles   to fill them
               with stain and stench

       what the Mopoke say
don't need saying
if you grown up under his eyes

now here's the part
you write Black Snake down
for a dilly of national flair
       true god you don't know how wild I'm gonna be
       to every fucking postmod blinky bill
       tryna crack open my country
       mining in metaphors
       for that place you felt *felt* you
           somewhere in
           the royal national

Waagan says use heart
but I am rage and dreaming
at the gloss-green palm fronds
of this gentry aesthetantique
       all this potplanting in our sovereignty
       a garden for you to swallow speak our blood

if you're taking that talk
you gotta scrape it from my schoolhouse walls
filter gollywog ashtray snugglepot kitsch
into your pastoral deconstruct
       fill four'n twenty pies
       with artisan magpies
       if you sever their heads
       you can wear them to the doof

I say rage and dreaming
for making liar the lyrebird
for making mimetic
the power   Baiami gave
when Ribbon's mischief swallowed first life
       ochre dust
       creation breath
       ancestor song

we aren't here
       to hear you poem
you do wrong   you get wrong
you get
gobbled up

The Last Endeavour

And it was from each to each that ghosts grew boats: tree
spectre stacked sliced for belief and buoyancy to break
waves against the encroachable unknown. They gathered in
eachother's names, the botanist captain astronomer, their
lips blessed with blood and coal, each with boast of seal-
touched hands. Their bounty a sacrament fixed in mass
of covert cartography, vows buried in chasmic holds and
hearts. Spilling maps as they went from fair isle through a
sea of bright broken ends, waking new heaven, new earth.
Tell us, spake the kings and queens, tell us how far is the
sun from the deep of the sea, where lacks the vulture's
eye and Ethiopian topaz, where are the shoals of thunder
wrapped, and leviathan's harvest sewn, and where will
goodness be found? The morning star gazed down the
bowsprit and turned her back to leave. No matter no mind,
the sailors told sailors, as the ship heaved from the shore,
first to split sea and then sky. No matter what minds us we
have the promise of history, the order to bring light to the
dark. The captain from fair Albion set loose on those wide
oceans with grasping trident gaze, a head of shark's teeth,
a spine of swallow's breath, desire the wind behind sails.
They moved in voyage, the moon pulling at wave as the
star raced from the ship. Now the rage, the law, the strange
coast of Calais and the coming again of that whale dream to
split their nights in twain. From the bow the captain called
to storm, let this we gather make strong the steeple, make
swell the anthem. Let us break wave so bold the sea shall
remember the path, let us make these heavens learn.

It was true they had left with orders, with chronometer, ammeter and altimeter, with compass and astrolabe, with a box for heads and a hull of ghosts. It is true the ship grew restless, as the botanist plucked cormorant and butterfly from the air, and the astronomer was caught nightly climbing the foremast to reach their star. It is true the sailors grew suspicious of the seal, packed so tight beneath them amidst sextant and sandglass, the entry guarded by the spectres that had been snatched from the wastes and hollows to rustle in cage and chain. As they spiralled sun, as their star slipped back to the ether, as their bellies grew heavy with salt water, the word began of why they had been sent. The sailmaker swore it was to gather gold, the midshipmen claimed it slaves. The cook reminded them that they were in flight of starpath after all, and what more might a king want than the light of heaven for their own keeping? The marines, who had been tasked with the ballast watch, believed it was to find the deepest sea cavern from which they might recover the dead. You each and all are fools, said the surgeon, rising from his rooms in the blood of the last soul to sip too much of sea. We go in search of the great southern land, of the lost eden, of the darkest abyss where we might release the ghosts. We are on a journey with no return so they will not find theirs back.

And sudden, a terror a terror a terror. The ship in violent cry, the night in roar, the hull in tear on the Coral Sea. The sky tipped in wide despair as the seamen clutched the railings. What now says the star, called the cook, as the heavens turned their gaze. What now says the sea, cried the marines, while the officers scrambled to their posts. Every trapping of cannon and ballast was spilt, every albatross and shriek

bridled to the deck. They discarded cloth and meat and
anchor to the reef as the great dark waters rose around them.
The captain charged from his chambers, his face wet with
wine, his gaze blurred with gulls. Men, men! he bellowed.
This is all a challenge of conviction, all a matter of belief!
Go forth to the depths and patch this gape with your hands,
we shall not give this endeavour to the deep.

The men scattered through the structure, each to swallow and
spit out as much sea as their lungs might bear. The botanist
called for the birds to beat their wings bolder, the astronomer
at the tip of the mast for their star to grace them in her reach.
Still the captain called from the crow's nest, this sea we
sail, this sea we split, this sky we break through like a babe
breaking shell, we have already done what could not be done!
We have moved boats eternal, we have dragged bodies to the
edge of history, we are coming and there is nothing but sky to
hold us! Shall we not betray our mouths to the vulgar taste of
peace, let us never know a garden yet to chart!

The night spent and so did the sea. Man could be noble like
this. Thirty sailors gave their lives to the ship that gave its
name to the strait that split it. They plugged the hole with
oakum and coral, with good men and noble dreams. They
lost the sextant and the artificial horizon, the rigging and
the mead, and the cargo guard reported six spirits short.
But the greatest grief was this: the seal that had sunk on the
southern coast, the orders that had by Deus vult sent them
to tabula rasa, the instructions for the end of the earth. The
captain was wild with grief, throwing net and line out to
the depths to drag forth his command. Bring me your star
magician, charge me your fish farmer!

This was the wreck that met the bay: the sullen silence of the wrathful spirit haunting the troubled deep. The wind held herald, the tide held slave, the looming shadow of a master of no domain. What now, what now, the captain called to the shore. Nigh two turns round the sun for this place, nigh death and disease and destruction for this isle. What command can have given you to me, what order for your end. We have cartographied historic what we have broken free from language, we have named you in our tongue.

The land refused. The ship roared. What dare is this rebuff, what insolence this denial. The captain the botanist the sailors all struck forth on their boats to fix their tablets to the bark. Strike axe and cheek, to the bone the blood the belief. We gave you what we came for and we demand it back for the soil. God was nothing to what we could imagine him, and this land is nothing to what we could make of it. The botanist broke off in search for the tree with the ship's wood-carved frame, the blossoms in want of poetry. The stargazer held back to fix the sky, to mouth the names of the big light and the little. But the captain would have nothing if he couldn't take it. They cried out to unrelenting night, this land is ours of the South, of the Sea, of the Never-Never, of the Harmless Eden. Yours to the Ending, the Desert, the Nulla Nulla, the Vanished Tribes of the Soothed Pillow in the Dying Race. We will not suffer silence, we will not leave unknown.

Through the dark rung weeping as the astronomer lost his star once more to the southern sky, the wide deep that wanted nothing of him. While the seamen scrambled the shore, the ghosts slipped their spectres. They waded the gentle roll of wave to the sand and tested their flushing fingers through the foam. Too good, too good, this eloquent offering of birdcage to gulls. Too good this waiting casket.

The cove broken up by roars and calls, the spirits beset the bay, while the ship swallowed the dark.

SPECTRE

Acknowledgement of Cuntery

I would like to acknowledge
And pay my respects
The past the present emerging
        ; Country ; Elders ; Care ; Custodians
I welcome you all
You all like me
To the unpronounceable the
Unrememorable time immemorial
Would like to would like   acknowledgement
Invitation/invite you all
To be acknowledged
And welcome invitation and respects
To any Indigenous past present
Emerging now watching me acknowledge
To be acknowledged with my respects and my conciliation
After the show during the show during acknowledgements
As I regard Indigenous with glances with acknowledgement

I would like to say sovereignty and reconciliation
I would like sovereignty and reconciliation

        I would like to say
Deadly gubba blackfella mob gammon sis
Would like to speak the unpronounceable
To say your name your nation again again
Correct at last when compact
Would like to acknowledge my school trip to Alice
Respect humble unliveable unimaginable

Respect those black boys in Alice
Except for those black boys in Alice
        Except for Alice

I would like to wear your flag
On shirt and tote and Facebook filter
I would like to graffiti your suburbs   with your flag
Would like to ask you about the constitution
Would like to acknowledge that I am asking
I would like to acknowledge the decades of struggle
From communities I don't drive through
I would like to blame you for your vote
And apologise that I didn't bring enough flyers
To your suburbs   to your homes
I would like to be invited to your homes
To pay my respects my   acknowledgements

I would like all this acknowledged
And to remind everyone
That we are meeting on Land Stolen
        and remind everyone how sad it is
        you all died
To remind everyone
        that you're all dead
        or stolen
        or silent
How sad   it is

I would like r e s p e c t and
                a c k n o w l e d g e m e n t
For all this respect and acknowledgement

The Trope Speaks

The trope neatly folds conflictual narratives of national subjectivities and external politics into aesthetic production.

The trope styles itself as the working-class battler as it navigates economic, geographic and cultural displacements.

The trope stages forbidding tales of estrangement and annihilation against the backdrop of a land fundamentally opposed to humanity and civilisation.

The trope feels a ghostly spectre haunting the land, but smothers it with fence and field and church.

The trope offers an aesthetic hybridisation of Eurocentric and Aboriginal culture wherein all that is fundamentally alienating to the white settler gaze is translated into jargon and misappropriated cryptomythology.

The trope cultivates themes of exploration, discovery, settlement and struggle which emphasise settler heroism and resourcefulness to assert a right-to-dwelling against the unheimlich of the land.

The trope plants graves in the pastoral scene and sees the flicker of white skin passing through the trees.

The trope sucks at the longneck and tells you that you'll be joining the hunt tonight.

The trope wants Australia like a man wants a woman, he fairly trembles with wanting.

The trope once had long hair and spoke of liberation, but now votes for local conservatives and owns a boat.

The trope, according to legend, can be found in lakes, swamps, pools and billabongs, and is said to make a loud booming noise when it leaves the water at night in search of little boys and girls to swallow.

The trope is available for purchase in a wide range of hand-dyed linens.

The trope sleeps in a homestead built over bones.

The trope contracts, its planks creak, but its grandfather built it to last and it knows its roofs and verandahs will give just enough to survive unscathed.

The trope thinks every tree is a ghost gum.

The trope has run and run for miles to get a bottle of eucalyptus oil from Dr Owl.

The trope sits on a solitary branch, white and stark against the sky, and has a gun.

The trope says hadn't we better turn back now, it's getting dark.

The trope imagines myths imagining myths imagining myths imagining myths.

The trope caresses you tender in the public bar, traces its sweaty hand over your brown skin and drags its fat tongue across your neck.

The trope doesn't love you; the trope doesn't even know your name.

The trope will meet you on the road. Kill him.

Guarded by Birds

When you go
as the spaces between
wine&zoloft
say you must

at thirty-seven
or some other too soon
before old has a chance to grow in you
before youth has time to loose you from his claws

      I will meet you at the edges of a body shaped like loss
      and trace the outline of your absence with smoke

                  then take from the air
            the name of a man
            who smelt like river
                  and spoke like distance

Second surviving son to two generations
of fathers to buried boys
      loved&beloved in your loudest lonely
by the daughter to what I swear
I heard you call   deliverance

                too goodtoo good
                this eloquent offering
                of birdcage   to gulls

There are knowings I cannot tell you
and things you do not know how to say
between tradition and trauma
there are nights when we meet voiceless
in the shadow of oncewas gum
   the memory of leaf and branch
   the place where you want to die

I know little of this ceremony
have only collected for the coolamon
carved from river red
to carry water to carry child to carry smoke
   to carry you to those who watch
   and hope there will be place for you

    When you go
      I will be the one to tell the birds
      they will wait as I gather the eucalypt

      and tell me

take them   still living
break the branch   if you must

To the Poets

Maybe what's been done to you has been done to me too?

When first and scared you knew only this place as hostile, as
wanting. You saw no marks of yourself here. The horror slips
sublime as you build house and fence and church. The first
axe to strike the gum. You can look upon a wilderness if
you think there's a homestead to return to, that there will be
crop and meat and cloth to harvest. You spread it and sprawl
it and sing it back for the common wealth, taking and
making words to diffuse the harsh edges of language over
animal vegetable and mineral. You ferment myth into the
bush and the billabong to give yourself history, and there's
enough there to make a man and call him native born.
Our bones mortar your buildings, your poems, but all the
while we're away in fringes and reserves. Don't look at me.
Cover up the earth that knows me but leave wells so you
can drain it. Take our language from our bleeding mouths
and give it to your songs. All of this to keep giving him
sounds to speak himself as something separate from whence
he came. When he grows up and forgets what was lost from
him, you'll remember this birth fondly, you'll wear it on silk
frocks and hang it from your ears.

These pastoral poems play in the field but don't enter the
house. They might burn down the homestead but they never
sleep in it with a cousin's foot against your spine on the
living-room floor after bathing off the mud in two inches of
tank water, belly full of charcoaled meat. They don't watch
them cut into turf and pasture from within: remembering

before fence and field but still feeling the loss of something you've known. You cannot redeem the pastoral. You cannot kill it and wear its skin. You cannot put back into the earth what you've taken from it. You've disturbed the ancestors. The words are wounds and that's done now. Accept it. Learn it anew. I've had enough of your grief and your potplanting in our land. These are the dreamings we have now. Did you listen? Do you understand that the land doesn't need any of us? I know this pride. My Elders taught me their names. Warned me of Tiddalik and Gongarra and told me where we'll go when they come back.

Do you know what I am, what I move between? Do you know the light I have looked upon in the crest of morning? Do you know what has watched me in dusk and dark? Do you know what lores I have had to learn while you play in everything they protect? Do you know that none of the trees your poems bleed are ghost gums? Do you understand that when you write the kangaroo the wallaby the bilby the bandicoot the cockatoo the blacksnake the waterlily the brush the bush the sapling the ghost gum that you are puppeting your hands through ancestors, through relations?

D, I wanna go home but I don't know where home is. I'm walking through this country I've never not known, this country you've told me to never walk at night. I've been driving along the river so deep in the dark because I'm trying to hear them say my name like they used to. I never want to go away from here. I never want to turn on my phone, I never want to slide up the highways that they're rolling out over our valley to learn all the ways it was carved up in their words. D, I don't know our words I want but I

know I don't want to meddle with approximations. D,
I want to come home and I want my bones to recognise it.

I'm no better than the pastures and I'm no better than the
poems made from them. I'm no better because I'm black
and I'm no better because we moved to the nice side of the
reserve, got our own rooms and a pool. None of this is to
say that I'm wiser or more present here. It's to say that I'm
tired, that I want nothing more than to go home and sink
and sleep and dissolve, and home is something more to me
than it might be to you.

My old people are getting old and I'm getting scared. I want
anger noble, but I always knew poetry was mostly there
to protest the poets. The world is sick with empty words.
I have all the theory in the world to explain the logics of
our erasure, the violence of our replacements and our more
palatable Others. I've read the work done to demonstrate
how this literature triangulates our elimination against
the archipelago where you move to your innocence. But
no-one's ever asked how we are both colonised by and
inheritors of these words. J asks – what is a world, and what
does it mean to end it? I want to know what it means to lose
the world you're still standing in.

decolonial poetics (avant gubba)

when my body is mine i will tell them
with belly&bones
>   do not touch this prefix
>   or let your hands burn black
>   with your unsettlement
>   there are no metaphors here

when i own my tongue i will sing
with throat&finger
>   gobackwhereyoucamefrom
>   for i will be
>   where i am for

when i am aunty
i will say, jahjums,
>   look what we made for you
>   look at this earth we cauterised
>   the healing we took with flame
i will show them a place
they will never have to leave

and when i am dead
they
>   will not
>   say   my name

and when you are dead,
>   you can have poems

Concessions

It's been a while since I've walked through a house that rattled with me, peeled a mug of milky bushels from a plastic tablecloth and watched moorhens scratch air outside a shed spilling rusted parts and dusty dogs. It's been a while since I've chopped wood or checked a back fence, and longer since I've taken water for the calves or chooks. Some of it is probably still there: the birdbaths of crumbling cement, the hot sick smell of mouldy bread, the faded black paint on the dolls' faces and the coiled carpet snake in the shed by the aviary. She loved birds, but I never asked her how. Just soaked up the heat from the wood burner in the kitchen, just splashed in the third-filled tub with a cousin or two, just leant against the fence as the caw of silhouettes descended across the dam. There's no stars like the ones that hang wide night above that dam. I'll never be old enough for the verandah, or to drive the basher to the back. We watched VHSes on a TV that always needed a minute to warm up, drinking expired soft drink from the fridge out back and fighting for who got to sit in Pa's good chair. Mum's shoulders took two hours to ease on the drive home, and Dad was always rotating two or three of us out of the house so it wouldn't shake. In another version of history we are here, together, still: the cattle and the dogs, the birds and the silhouettes, the dam and the damned. In this I watch old movies and try to catch a glimpse of us in the hot brown blur of a screen, that broad voice, that shimmer of sweat, that work-scarred hand curled around an always-too-warm beer. History forgets some places, and stutters on new ways to name old ghosts. There's more than asbestos rotting in these walls. But I would give most things to read the careful way you spelt our names above the phone, or to watch an afternoon sink across the dam. To sit on the verandah and hear you tell me about the birds.

Bad Taxidermy

The brushtail dyed Tesco ice-chocolate brown and face stuffed forehead high like a squirrel.

The tour that I left five minutes into the guide recounting all the middle names of its benefactors.

Every street name the same here as it is at home.

The quoll tail pulled out taut and haunches raised to best recall the common red fox perched in prey of the squirrel.

Kylie Minogue in hotpants and a hot-pink koala knit sitting side-saddle on a scribbly with a lush bluegum arrangement.

Whoever named the Tasmanian Devil, and the faintly otter-like lift of his small dark paws on the acrylic shelf.

The Instagram ad for Australian Native Birthflower charms and corresponding zodiac chart of symbolic meanings they are said to manifest.

The Welsh newsreader stumbling over the names of towns turned kindling.

Every photo of our shoes I've taken accidentally and then found on my camera roll but not deleted.

The £17 sacks of organic goon at Marks & Spencer.

The way the storm's mist looks almost like the smoke I can still taste from here. The fear that my lungs have collected enough to exhale and stain the air.

The swamp wallabies of the Jardin des Plantes with fur darker than they've ever needed back home.

Angling my reflection out of photos of cabinets with drawings of my ancestors rubbing sticks.

The lungfish nailed to a birch board and the sea shanty I wait for him to sing.

The thin white eucalypt splitting the path at Dublin Zoo.

The man laughing in the anthropology museum and the sleeve
I wiped my nose with after telling him to fuck off.
The eBay bidding war over Kylie's hot-pink koala knit.
The Facebook ad for canine air-pollution masks and all the people
tagging each other in the comments.
The row of crocodile skulls arranged like a butcher's window.
The koala in the museum bleached white from flash photography
and the plastic citrus leaves he sucks.
The cabinet of Pacifica statues posed in worship around a bowl of
coins marked 'anthropologist fundraising ritual'.
The unfair green of organised countryside.
The spare cabinets waiting in anticipation in the extinction room.
Photos of our feet walking through the colony's churches while all
ours burn.
The tangled echo of children and gulls laughing in the university's
stone square that rattles like a magpie, sung through a lyrebird.

Bread

They announced the end of the buildings where
we might stumble surprised unprepared into embrace
your afternoon clear my ass bare beneath my skirt a

city park uncompromised by memory or state violence
they announced they'd be closing down the city but not
the violence   they said it on the radio where I sat at

my desk my bits shaved for the pleasant unexpected they
announce the shift to purpose to intentional attending
say it's only a matter of time for the bush the bar for

every external to collapse into privacy excluding resource
extraction so now there's no soap left in the world and
all the poets have fallen into weeping. they're calling us up

on the phone   asking for arguments I have nothing
for the paper the anthology   nothing to make a moment
to rally, just bread. is it blak bread, bush bread, is it small

business sole trader bread, is it oppressed bread. I say it's not
even sourdough because my starter grew mould. they want
my anger humble righteous noble,   want blak bread and

roses, want to sell papers with my quote, my photo warm
filtered, my crisis bread available   for limited release.
I want an afternoon with you, stumbled surprise, no violence,

no humble righteous noble,   not even asking for much.

Stutter

Hold the body   the baby   the urge
        to hold that stutters muscle
        that cradles warm air
crush yours into mine to tell me what I'll miss
    the way you move through a room

give me proximity like a threat then give it
again so I'll remember it real good

I like best to find me suggestive
like best the self   to let you move into what's left
like it best when you can't tell me anything
it's best when I want into dark
                    what I don't have to say aloud

there's nothing to say but
            to bring to the room a mercy of limbs
I came to give your hands a burden
I came to your hands the cradle of wrist

it'll look good for me to look good doing that
            like it best like that like I let you do like I mean it
it's best if we only remember through the body
to build muscle around it before you go

the urge to reach you stutters   body
it speaks from the choke of my throat
don't let us let the air know   this is our most vulnerable
the crush of things   the proximity that might kill
       don't let the room empty before
              I've built the muscle to remember
don't go until I can like it like that

Moving Day

The roof has new cracks for the rain.

I'm angry you didn't put the buckets out fast enough, that the storm is soaking into your three identical pairs of brown boots. I'm worried the dog might try to lick at the carpet and the whole flat smells like an old shed. I make tiny angry noises in the hall while you drink coffee making tiny morning noises and let me be.

You're wearing pants but are still in assemblage, breaking into consciousness and its responsibilities. Buckets are not the priority. I'm angry but I kiss your head because I'm trying to understand buckets are not a priority and they're your shoes to soak. You sip more coffee and remind me to drink the tea you left me by the bed.

If I explain being angry I might cry. I hate crying over buckets or carpets or shoes. The first time I cried in front of you I couldn't explain why the slant of light through the living room split me so much, and you held me gentle with my face against the lounge because I didn't want you to see me.

You don't understand it, but you have been generous to my every form of anxiety with the proviso I don't hold you responsible to realities I make in margins.

Sometimes you're frustrated that I tell stories in circles and can never answer a question straight.

Sometimes you're frustrated that I buy too many things I don't use.

Sometimes you're frustrated that I have threatened to skulldrag so many of your exes.

Sometimes you're frustrated that I baby you but don't take appropriate measures of self-care.

The smoke filtered through the cracked window and settled over the damp carpet while we were gone. This room smells as old as it is.

You don't mind but I do – I mind everything. When we're packing I want to tell you how you'll like the garden, to bring you things you don't need, to ask if you're angry with me.

You interrupt the clamour of boxes and bags and ash rising from the stained carpet to smile every time I think I will, and the dog curls around our feet every time we pause.

I got everything I wanted but forgot the words I learnt for it.
Baray-gir.
You are other things than what you give me, but
Baby boy.
My love my love my love,
slipping new words into the old grammar in search of ways to call you.

Some of this is just playing at peace and sharing desks at the apocalypse. Some of this is rearranging rooms against anxiety and packing boxes for worlds I'm not ready to meet.

I'm ready for you in the same way my mouth is sometimes ready for the last gulp of tea that I forgot still pooled in the mug. The way songs pause in me interrupted and wait days until I can listen to the end.

The poem says you do not have to be good, and you tell me that not all days will be.
Mostly I'm tired of myself and of the work of being, so I leave loving you to muscle memory.

I think that's probably bad.

You think we're okay, and I should let us practise at peace.

The dog likes to hold our fingers in her mouth so we might ease the strain of new teeth breaking gum. You let her gnaw your hand, you tell her she's fine, she's fine, she's fine.

With Hidden Noise

THIS BURNT-OUT NEON THRONE IS A CABINET
OF CODES FROM THE SECOND-HAND FIRESELLER
TO THE SEA // IT'S FINE AND CHEAP AND HERE
HE CALLS TO THE NIGHTS THAT DESERTS
PROVIDE // THE BOX SPLITS AND DISCARDS IN
HEAT AND THE HORIZON FLICKERS WITH THE
SIGNS OF THE DEAD // I'VE GOT PLENTY I'VE
GOT SO MUCH HE SAYS AND THE NIGHT WINKS
BACK TO HIS ONLY // SO WHERE FROM WHICH
OR SHORE CAN I OR YOU OR YOU IN YOU DRAG
FORTH A FUCKING DRINK //

I'VE GOT PLENTY AND SO MUCH A ROCKET A
DEAL A JAR IN A HEART // THE NICEST NOTHING
YOU'LL NEVER OWN // A BODY ECSTATIC AND
THE GUN THEY BREAK IT WITH // THE SONG
I STRIPPED FROM THE STREETSIDE HOWL //
BEHOLD THE UTILITY OF AN IDEA YOU CAN'T
LOOK IN THE EYE //

where from here my belated beloved i moved antipodes for
you or you // there's dust on the shelf but antigone tells me
i'm barely starting // out of booze and barely starting // what
did you even or ever and however did you dare // they're
closing the bars in kamberra and there are bars in kamberra
// there are evers and they refuse the sky to land // and for
heaven say heaven for world say I bought it //

THE PORCELAIN THE ZYGOTE THE TWINE
DRAINING DRAW HERE BROUGHT ALL FOR THE
SHOW // GIVE ME MY VIRUS AND FOREVER // A
SANDCASTLE TO KICK // GIVE ME A SALE ONLY
I CAN DEPRAVE // IT'S A BARGAIN A STEAL A SIN
TO IMAGINE YOU INFINITE OF INSTALLATION //
TO READ THIS POEM TO YOUR HOLOGRAM // TO
MAKE THE WORLD COME IN MY WAY

Mrs Kookaburra Addresses the Natives

Humans! Please be kind
      to all Bush Creatures™
      and don't pull flowers up by the roots.
And please be gentle
to Little Ragged Blossom
of blessed tender heart
loved beloved by Bush and its Folk
a wee speck of blushing babe
      of lovely important sadness©

We mustn't forget Little Obelia! Held in guard
by athousands of rainbow fish
      and a charming seaweed estate.
She is a shiny white pearl burst open
near the pleasant size of Little Ragged Blossom
who goes oft to visit her in the sea.

Humans! You remember how on the killing
      of the wicked Mrs Snake
      The Bush™ became joyful, and
      rich Mr Pilly, the father of Lilly Pilly the actress
      gave a dinner party at the Gum Inn?
Such festive spirits we were in and against
as Snugglepot and Cuddlepie held corrobboree
for the native bears at White City®
                 (which the evil wicked Banksia Men
                 call Korijekup
                 a foul old word
                 we don't say here).

Humans, now tell me:
>Do you really think all the bad Banksia Men
>were deadibones when they went to the bottom
>of the sea in the great fight with Mr Lizard and Mr
>Eagle and Cuddlepie?

>Not deadibones, not a bit!
For it was just last Cheap Tuesday
at Lilly Pilly's Picture Palace
that the nasty dark and dry cones
burst terrible into the room.
Snatching up Nittersing and Narnywos and Jindyworobak
perhaps in revenge of Mrs Snake
or her aunt and mother-in-law and three cousins.
And surely would have gobbled them whole
were it not for Mr Lizard and brave and strong Nuttybub!

How blessed we are
in This Delightful Bush™
>which lends its dappled light
>to our important tales
>so that we might share with our little nuts
How frightened we were
of those straggly, godless fiends.
>>What fun it was
>>to see their eyes plucked out
>>by those fearsome redtail cooks
>>that they called
>the foul old word
>we don't say here.

Hold

Holding loud night
for a moment
        thinking of the word for moon
        in the language I didn't know
        when I came here last
        we have nothing to say to each other
        except everything

I know these trees
by the throat
but there's new leaves
for the horizon to halo
to slice that last little light on your face
for the last offerings
before the streetlights start
to splutter the dark

I should take responsibility
and you said you were going to be kind
are you breaking the past enough
have I buried enough dead
not all that haunts is ghost
and I'm sorry to be so living
        so loud
so tell me why you dragged me into this

done, and gone
and grown
not all that holds must hurt
this night has no room
        for more dusk

but hold it   still
a little longer
a little warm a little care   still
like the edge of afterglow
the scatter of sunset
the not here,
the not now,

            let none of this run parallel
            just soft, let it sleep
                    there's enough light
                    out there

In Fright

fuck it, there's worse things than crying in a conference paper,
like every time I can't breathe becomes last words, the sea
swallowing a homeland, like a pipeline splitting sovereign soil.
I hope this email finds you holy. I'm drafting in the notes app at
the back of a reading, I dressed my best westfield vogue, my too
careful chic, if I sound short it's because these four lines took nine
weeks. the host said byo compulsions so I've got a framework to
hover round the room. it's like an empty glass you carry back to
the bar, a projector streaming burnt desert holograms against a
grotty warehouse wall, a UE boom stuttering out that
    all the little devils are proud of hell.

I hope this email finds you aching. in a competition for who
can look most laconic my mouth is never relaxed enough for a
smirk. the virus missed me to strike a child starving someplace
closer than I want to know, the phone is buzzing and everyone is
cancelled, some white girl in a bedazzled *homewrecker* bomber is
writing a memoir and the war will end when we splinter in heat
death. best wishes, you're the only man I'll ever let touch me, the
nightmare is the closest I ever get to history, and after careful
reflection I realise I never learnt how to pray. I think it'd look like
the leadlight waterlily mum made for the bathroom, smell like
a bandaid, sound like we haven't had a storm this bad since you
took out that tender ship of mine. my poems are lacking shade
and brine, are recipes for things that will one day kill me. at least
we're lucky to have jobs, at least they only raised the rent once.
sign off and say you love me enough to let this disappear. say keep
safe, say the worst thing we did was tell ourselves there would be
memories.

DEBRIS

Dirge

the other history
        is a dream we tell
to give the night ghosts

to run our blood, think of homes
we won't build, tease children
        that won't warm by the fire

        we will not raise bioluminescent angels
lucky to be suckling bull kelp in the teeth of sea
you'll never teach them to ride bicycles through tar sands
I won't crochet extinct totems on their masks

a different kind of barren to imagine
a centre we knew wouldn't hold
        it could have been
        and we gave it a go

what's the point of trading names
        to the end of the world
if you give me a ring make it hollow

To the Parents

I'm writing this book in the shadow between deaths. I live in middle place. In country that I must care for but that doesn't suit the colonial appropriation of our ancestral. Between totem and cryptomythology, between native and notfor.

After work J and I go back to his apartment in the outer-inner-west. It's the charming sort of dilapidated, where most of what is claiming back the crumbling stone is pretty and green, wrapped around a done-it-yourself balcony where we feed the brushtails and water the currawongs and listen to the angophora dance heavy limbed in the wind. It feels enclosed and away, but never quiet. Shapes flicker corner-eyed and mirror-edged here like the streetlights smudged by the jacaranda weeping through the garden wall. The cat only knows how to scream. J talks to the lorikeets that crowd on the windowsills he's lined with seed. We're curled here in the safest site of our everyday struggles with infinitude. At this distance we can justify all manner of intellectual and cultural isolations. We write poetry here, and about here.

Twenty minutes or so on the old Koori road they keep paving over til I'm back on the M4, on my way home to endlessly trace more footsteps between my bed and the bush, to get the last bit of the story before I can finish this. Traffic stacks up outside the Institution where a single gum sprawls its pale arms up to the sky. South Creek is running low and dry, and my uncle up at the farm says

he's had to sell off the cattle that he can't afford to feed.
I go the tree-lined road and drive slow for the dusking
roos bounding into the ironbarks. Every few seconds is a
flicker of scribbly gum, white and stark and inscripted in
the distance. Mum and Dad have just come back from
a community meeting – there's spagbol on the stove, the
jack russell bounces back-leggedly at the screen door, and
the blue heeler is watching patiently at the back. The sky is
vermilion behind black silhouettes. The walls are lined with
family photos and the decades of Mum's cross-stitching that
she made for the childhood room where we would curl in
each other's beds to hear stories of our bush friends – Blinky
Bill, Snugglepot, Cuddlepie, pastoral homesteads, native
florals and bush bandits. There's more in the shed, and
more again in my car. My baby book features a charmingly
chubby, blushing knock-off May Gibbsesque babe playing
cheerily with a young brushtail beneath my names and
descriptors – Evelyn (for my great-grandmothers) Araluen
(for waterlilies) Anne (for habit) Corr (for the Irish refugee,
for the mission worker, for the absences of history by which
a name will refuse to abandon whatever it can claim). Hair,
dark. Complexion, dark. Eyes, dark. Folded inside is my
first fat-faced photo, my birth certificate, and my Common
Seal Confirmation of Aboriginality (for convenience, in case
of fire).

Here's the entanglement: none of this is innocent and
while I seek to write rupture I usually just rearrange. I can
name the colonial complexes and impulses which structure
these texts but it doesn't change the fact that I was raised
on these books too. They tell me they never chose them to
hurt us, and I never thought they did. History is a narrative

and they did everything they could to write a new one for us with whatever tools they could find. They both grew up surrounded by the bush in country New South Wales towns. None of my grandparents finished school and they all had very low levels of literacy. Books were one of the many things my mum never had growing up but made sure to give her children. She chose them for us around what we could afford, but always looked for stories of the bush she knows and loves with intimate detail. She read them to us with care and patience, even in all the years she was working two jobs to put those books in our hands. Her hands ache every night from years of labour that began at a sheep station at eight years old. Each night after work she sews us quilts with native floral prints, cuts stained glass to give us windows of our totems, cross-stitches gumnut patterns to hang in whatever houses we might one day live in. She named us each so tender, with such vision of the home she will never stop making for us.

Dad remembers having books – a few from his parents, and some from a teacher boarding in the same house when he was a child in Penrith. She shared the colonial books that he would go on to read to us with salt grains and disputations. He built word-worlds of fae and foe in both the forest and the bush. As a child, I enjoyed those stories. I enjoyed the lands they peered into, the adventures they described. He made room enough for us to scribble our own stories into their pastures. He taught us how to care for our country, but he let us learn how to love it. I missed all this nuance and allowed myself to think we were losing to the settlers when I discovered theory. I learnt new words to write down and explain everything that I felt departed from my notions of the Authentically Aboriginal. The books, the cross-stitching, the childhood home bursting at the seams with national ephemera they had collected over the years.

It was an easy sort of antagonism, where I could see my parents as the victims of a colonial condition, and not agential selves who had sacrificed everything to give us something. A tidy narrative that forgot the decades of work they did writing curricula for Aboriginal education across New South Wales, creating programs to bring Elders into schools, developing resources for communities to address drug abuse through cultural learning and safety, going to meetings and bushcare, picking up the pieces, being there to remind and remember. Dad tells me that these were the stories told to stop kids like him from dying and disappearing into the bush, to the closed fist of the state. His story will never fit into a poem. It's too heavy to dangle from an ear.

While my siblings and I consumed those stories, we were never taught to settle for them. My parents never pretended these books could truly know country or culture or me – but they had both come from circumstances in which literacy and the access it affords was never a given. They just wanted me to be able to read.

I unpack the car and everything spills out, back to where it belongs. No reconciliation, no rupture, just home.

Wangal Morning

sounds almost mute
like earth
like blood
then heat
move in shadows   slow given back light
measure   the measureless
once more around time

fracture sound
      half sigh
      fill sky
gather old light
from other place
when we,   new
      muted
you, gentle
slipping through horizons
for birdsong
for your poems
for what you have buried here
give these offerings
say to dawn
      make light soft
      make light gentle
      make it not a night
      split open
let not this night
      split me open

I'm still asleep
but you know I will wake
if you need

Home, After the Fire

I haven't been smoked since Nan died
it's not the blood or the ceremony
that's been bleeding me these months:
      I've slept in seven houses
      and I didn't take my hair back to burn

I'm on the way home now
with a bag of ashes to unpack
there's a windowsill of pepperberry
I lined out to dry
there's blossomseeds I planted here
      before I left
it's gonna take some nights
to learn to sleep the scrub again
to gather enough sunslip for my belly
to wash my skin back into its scent

I've never lived to see a home become a ruin
just watched all this roadside flame
waiting in smoke shrouds
      for news for the house for my dogs for Dad
we return differently when we're made to leave
we ghost hands where furniture hasn't stood in years
pause in corners
hold doors and linger   like the smoke scent
I try not to move immemorial with my shoes on
I've never lived nowhere   no other way

we'll do it again in our voices
the first thing is to gather – be it fallen or snapped
it must be green fresh, almost wet:
>   we're not here to disintegrate
>   we're here to dissolve flesh to air
>   to shed spirit from body or house or grief
>   to dance at our most visible
>   and then put everything back in its place

no bodies walk innocent here
and no body's gonna hold me in if I need to go
no smoke detector, no hostile house
could keep out my ancestors if they want me   and
there's nothing I won't say if I'm afraid

but I don't feel like it's time to lose her
or the house or the farm or the dam
when I'm ready to mourn
I'll take the highway to the rivermouth
go north through the sandstone walls
drive west as the scrub sinks the swamp
offer passage for every cousin or crow
I might pass on the way
>   play the radio when I get there
>   trail the smoke from my skin

The Inevitable Pandemic Poem

It's April and the city is walking
gentle dogs and sanguine children
the light yellow and soft translucently through gum
the Dan Murphy's car park full
and every verandah dangling drunk acquaintance

it's April and everyone is home
but the city left its lights on
the horizon blinking at us from the bottom of the hill where
we stroll lanes and backstreets with the other gentrifiers
everyone competes for the best rescue story
as our dog licks shit stuck to stray browning leaves

April is a spilt month
leaking from the edges of pre-faded posters reading
we're all in this together
emails from universities that can't pronounce my name
asking if I've ever heard of AbStudy or the dole
it's the warm sour smell of the starter I couldn't get to rise
the job of whoever had to take down the swings
from the playground that is best done under cover of night
the faint hum of the laptop that's been running since summer
and the corner of the home I can't go back to
where the reception is clear enough for my parents
to hear me when I call

it's April and Apple had the heartwarming footage
ready for the master cut, Apple has a cave under the sea where
they store the apocalypse, to roll it out between flashes of
cooking tutorials for meals I'll never make
it's April and the government is selling Anzac Day on
YouTube, like a promise they can't remember breaking

I am wearing April like luxury loungewear, strolling
from bed to bedside in a tangle of phone chargers a
crown of empty mugs the endless of an abandoned promise
the always of emails answered in another's sleep
the readiness to never surface from the dark

it's April and it's my job to pack poems for the
flameproof bunker, to write the one that will sit
on top like the ancestral prologue for the nation
that carried on and did what it wanted anyway

mine is a letter to my Animal Crossing wife
to the crow scratching air on the highway side
to the family that I promised against history
I would never be made to part from

we all write our poems on masks
and now there are none left for the city

I am walking April with my dog
and she is so happy

Bahloo

I am watching you watch me
with light carried by voice gentle
      voice soft
voice to call all my world of sound of sight

bahloo
I have turned round the sun
turned in to you
left as much of my blood in the soil
as my blood is the soil

in tree hollow
above the stars
these crowded earths
press against the other
      as they always do
are flown between
in hum in caw in gahr
in spirit shard
      as you teach
in and against me where
I am never as small   as I remember

where I might wake cold
might wake quiet
might carefully make
      the life I don't get
      the home I don't know

or I can choose something else
and be it or not
but always answer the voice
     with always,
     I will be yours
     and carry yours

     sing it back
     slip crescent and wane
     like   fingers in my hair
     like   blood gift to soil
     like you made a star in her
     that mapped me to myself

bahloo
I am only edges at your light
and I thank you for your dew
for your pale face
how you dance upon the river
how you follow me home

K1: Yellomundee

Beyond your stage
the audience murmur
men and women weep
and silk their skin bare,
for here and gone and taken.
Held by mostly mountains
you wear crowns
of returning eucalypt:
I can't see your lashes
but feel them still soft
like that skin they try to skin
to wear you with words
and all them names they reason
and rub out.

All this might be lonely
unmarked and highwayside
but then the stars come here
to shine the shape of song
and hear you say
it's nice
to have someone
to talk to.

THE INLAND SEA

When we laughed the sea from the belly, the
country opened to drink. Nothing is forgotten from earth,
just moves in muscle memory, what doesn't echo is
recalled by the first bird to rustle free from the dust.

       Here is where we met the stars. Here is where
we sung their shadows through soil. We earnt back the water
and bathe in it under the eye of that which carved it through
the earth. Nothing like a river could be just for the name.
Nothing like a sea could leave without us knowing why.

///

///

So turn your gaze then; take the map from the wall and the
ash from the archive, from your mouth spit the pages you
mistook for law and see if they can cartograph a ghost. This
vision is the cleanest bloodshed imagined, staining and

       spilling stretched through bush and book alike.
A country only named as nation: a stage, a scene, a street to
stumble through breathless, melancholy, vast and vapid
pressed down by heat and light and all else left to cite.

The glistened decay that withers fragile delicate,
collapsing into the handsome arms of history. Curled by
invasive species it is windswept and crumbling to the sea. It
stands at the bow as the white sails flee and burns up at the
       slightest song of sun.

///

///

How many rivers sailed til the story can be settled sufficient,
how many churches carried up the creek, how much glass
for that little dark light, how many ships dragged to the
desert, how much sandstone has been reaped for the dust?

///

    They're dragging black bodies
    through the halls, shooting black bodies on
    the street, blood on the concrete the wattle
    the sheets.

///

Enough and plenty, enough and plenty. In the fresh and
the salt it spreads, it spills out from the belly of the greed
that took it from here. Enough to fill mouths and cups and
tubs where black bodies can splash in suds, can shimmer
up in the shore, can swim and drink the sun. More of that
than white sails splitting sea, more of the muscle than the
memory, more of the every before this unendling time. The
river is dry but not empty, the river knows how when what
now blinks in the sky carved it to the earth.

///

    Imagine imagining this hollow.

///

///

What did your ruin want with us anyway? Sydney is soft and
humid and dying, your ghosts lingering and unsettling ash
as they trace too close to the fire's edge. Your god was dead
before the nails, and the cross was bored of waiting for a
word, and what for?

He's tired and we're tired and the windowsills are tired, and
what do rocks wait for but sun, sun. Your ruined eden, your
golden hair in curl and conquest, left in the bed, the bush,
the inland sea, the sunburnt country. The prophecy was
pretty, but never yours to wear. The white sails split the sea
slower

than the songs sent for warning, slower than the river carver
carried it through coast. Through water that would wash the
salted linens soil stained and blood drained, bleached and
burnt and flooded by every half-cast dream, every gift from
yours to ours. The bush and book alight.

///

What more could it want but our empty? What more than a
howled horror in echo through the cityscape, the ring the
shine, the heaving word first sung to sails? What more than
dancing the ocean out of you, what more than giving sea
back to the wreck, what more than sinking ships?

///

///

The waves still break on the shore,
the bodies still break on the floor.

///

Fern Up Your Own Gully

Deep in the heart of the forest   there's a
magical world
          where wondrous creatures   plaaay the daaay
awaaay

And an unusual girl
dreams of faraway places   dreams of cassette radio
          of blond boys
of defensible monarchies
          is comfortable with poetic forms of entanglement
and likes the smell of eucalypt

When she flew where   no-one had flown before
          there were huge! discoveries!
she used her powers   (she has powers)
she rescued the blond boy   she rescued the forest
she is crowned in f l o w e r i n g b l o s s o m
                    and all other holy things

          Deep in the trees:
The orni-thorhyn-chus-ana-tinus sings affectation
the eyelashed mama roo opens her pouch
the koala collects   his gumnut coins   his
sugarbush comb
a fresh change of unmentionables   and they all swag
jollily off to the coronation

Just hop in that pouch, unusual girl
hop in the swag   this whole home waits
in handpainted frames of silk native frocks
          wear them to your reading
          wear wattles from your ears
it's all metaphor for   the beautiful thin white woman
whose body slides linenly through bush
          the notion that when my straggly brown strips from
          the tree
          it will be the smooth glow of ghost gum beckoning
can't be lyric if you're   flora, right?
can't be sovereign if you're   fauna, right?

Unusual girls fuck up their dendrology
cos they didn't come to bushcare
fern up the gully girls
go live those pastel bush dreams
while me and my ancestors sit   pissed swinging on
the verandah couch

RIGHT   WHERE   YOU   WROTE   US

Boab

Leaving from empty rooms we say it shouldn't be so simple
to drive between land and sea and arrive at something whole
the bracelet I've been weaving slides east to west on my dash
while we watch an eagle swoop patterns
                                        of this country's muscle
not threatened by transferral or transformation
            knowing what to take   and where to put it

there's nothing this page can do for the light slant
of a smoke-hazed sun   for the cockatoo sailing
through sky   while every road to home is burning
she isn't asking for a song   just water seed and branch
                        just rest
            but we drive wondering which of us
                            will write this poem first.

Breath

J plays the radio in the bathroom, so when the news reports
the next death it reverberates across tile and porcelain. They
say the fires have grown strong enough to create their own
weather systems, to draw down lightning from the smoke.
They say they picked a truck up in a tornado of flame
and tossed it down a mountain. Last year at the march
for Kumanjayi Walker, my nation danced for rain outside
Sydney Town Hall. An Uncle told us the ancestors were
angry, that they are reminding us what order looks like.
Watching the land burn feels like a test of how much I'm
willing to see avenged. I run the hotel bath and sit in more
water than we're allowed at home, watch my hair swirl in
dark tendrils around me. No-one has ever asked, but I'm
scared of the sea.

Floating at dawn on the North Atlantic Ocean, I walk the
length of the deck as the ferry sways beneath me. I wander as
if drunk from lounge to shop to cafeteria. A few passengers
are watching the TV absent-mindedly as the newsreader's
accent clips unfamiliar over the names of towns that I've
walked barefoot, country I've danced and swum and sung.
Here where I've slept in slips of morning light, there where we
drove wide nights under a river of stars. She calls it a forest
fire, and I watch as their mute faces are washed in orange
glow. A man leans against the counter where I stand, and
I want to say – that's my home, and it's burning. Do you
understand how much is alight? That we can't breathe?
I watch him watch expressionless before the story changes
to the sport and his head tilts, his gaze involved.

I've written poems about fire. I come from a culture of ancient knowledge of and relation with flame. We are each totemically designated through it, our nations are demarcated by our fire stories, by what each terrain needs. It has a place in our body, on the land we pattern with old and new growth to bring that which forages and that which preys. It's our job to know when the wind lifts, when the trees are ready to sigh. There's something intoxicating about air filled with the smoke of burning red gum. Fire breathes and expels air. It knows what to take, if you know what to give it.

I don't know the fire here. It's something to curl around in some building where some old name once took tea. I feel panic rise through me as we pass the pub along the River Liffey, patrons crowding the roaring chimineas while swans honk along the banks. I imagine coals spilling down the cobbled street, the night wailing with sirens. When I check the Fires Near Me app, it opens unmarked somewhere in the British countryside. It's the same notification tone as Dad's emails. We meet cold mornings in home's evening to tallies of the day's carnage, cold fingers scrolling across continents to find our towns. In a groupchat my siblings back home list the roads that are closed each day, sharing screenshots of maps and alerts as if we aren't always already watching, as if by sharing news we already know, we might be able to do something.

It follows us wherever we go. On the radio in the chemist while I'm pondering over candied flavours of fruits that are burning on the branch. In the hotel lobby as we wait to sleep off ten thousand miles. The attendant at the

emigration museum who hopes Ireland learns from our
mistakes in their next election. The butcher who repeats
horrible horrible horrible, the baker who shakes her head for
the koalas, the bartender who says that he's sorry as he pours
me a cider that tastes like cordial warmed from a southern
sun. I run out of synonyms for burning as I watch through a
screen, hear my mum's voice strain through my headphones.

Between Sydney, Qatar and Dublin, a clapstick stained with
ochre dust goes missing from my luggage. It was carved from
a mulga tree at the back of some distantly related uncle's
property in Brewarrina, the ochre from veins at the edge of
Dharug and Gundungurra country that I gathered on a drive
after last year's Hawkesbury NAIDOC. I'm hysterical at its
loss, I never wanted to come, I've never wanted to leave home,
there are clearly ancestors who don't want me here. What
if that tree is gone now? I wail in frantic emails to airport
security. What if the fire took it too?

With each day I learn new ways to feel unprepared.
Strolling through St Stephen's Green with no words for
how to greet the place, no names for the birds. The anxious
game of converting currency, the growing ache in my spine,
the piercing cold biting at bare ankles. In Oxford I get into
a shouting match with an old white man sniggering at a
Gamilaroi carving. In London we drag suitcases back and
forth through Hyde Park to find the basement we rented
cash-in-hand. I don't travel well when all I want is to be
home, useless and frightened with ash in my lungs. We sit
in Starbucks for three hours as we wait to take our train to
Cambridge, reviewing endless pitches to put words to things
we are not yet ready to speak: that it's gone too far already,

that every year more people will die, that some places will simply never recover. I've already spent a semester marking poetry and prose from students who will probably need to flee their homes in coming years. I've started a book which seeks to tease the icons of Australiana that have been so volatile to this country. They, too, are burning.

We came to talk about temporality, about literature, about the necessity of art in a time of crisis. Whenever I sit to draft remarks, to make a comment, I find myself searching for the balance between sorrow for the living, and willingness for the land to lose us for its own healing. We spent our youths imagining this kind of life, dreaming of ourselves as writers and thinkers who travel the world to tell stories. Being here tastes sour and hollow. This doesn't feel like writing – it feels like relic-making. What use is a poem in a museum of extinct things, where the Anthropocene display is half-finished? I couldn't free the shield, I didn't find the head. What use is witness at the end of worlds?

On Invasion Day, I stand in the stone walls of Cambridge University and the sharp call of Murrawarri mulga rings through the quadrangle. The clapsticks aren't done with me. They come back with new questions: if we are to go, who will care for our relations? Who will greet the trees, who will leave honey for the moon, who will pattern the land with flame?

In Singapore airport J disappears into the smoking room while I stand at our gate, reading a sign advising on health precautions for the virus that has just started to make the news. On the form they ask us to contact a hotline if we experience shortness of breath within fourteen days of our return. In a few months, another black man will die with 'I can't breathe' choked from his throat. We arrive home to a house filled with ash.

FOMO

tell daramulum im sorry
and then ask the trees why they let
      me leave

theyve been keeping me up now
teaching me how
to walk through darkness
once known   like light

always asking:
have you worked out
is it binang or toe or elbow?
which pound of flesh
is to carve
        leave to soak by the window
        watch shoot and bud crawl
        round lip of glass

where you coming home to tho?
your river dont go that far
from baryulgil to warrimoo
you keep sleeping where
that boondi will sweep you
and fill your lungs
with salt and sea

didnt go   to barrangal dyara
missed homeground/yabun/naidoc/corroboree
still wear that flag tho
still wear your snake
still rally and forum
like a bodys nothing but voice
like some sound is colourblind

come back once a week
got you believing in seven days
just to stand edgeways
trace yourself bird ways
like you just   flew south   flew west
        grew winter down
        like waterlily wings
        like gawura   swimming down to sandstone
        and you heard

we
are too young
for ruins

                gowaynow
                dont come back here
                no more

Secret River

They said the river would find us. Even as sunslip splashed
our gold bellies brown and our toes curled but never kept the
stripe spirit stones at the depths we dared each other to dive,
they knew the river would come. Knew how these waters had
anabranched their vesselled beginnings, breaking currents of
wisdom before brokeing the shores of settlements. No secret
but a sovereign river, the great swallower of structure colonied
out to cultivate in stolen sun. A river older than its ancestors
whose battle-veined stone bore waters deep through down,
who wait in cave and basin like the water waits to break what
dares to build, like this river waits to drink.

No secrets given by a sovereign river, no mercy to shore for
sure. Here deep the heap and crumble is a town dragged
down to pray, a labyrinth of rust for longneck and eel. At
first a clumsy cart, the broken boards of fence and bridge and
every other boundary thing, all carrion sunk to the always
river of ria. Here the schoolhouse has been tipped out brick
by brick and tumbles down drowned ridges, the barn has split
its stalls and shingles against the current which carried water
even when all the sky was ice. The church was all it chose to
swallow whole. Sandstone slanted and sidelying, glass cracked
darkly and doors both askew and astray. Every opening has
been speared with the slick limbs and boughs of the gum
which crucified this house of another land's dreaming.

Water carries immemorial, a river without peace will not let
you pray. The best way to learn a lesson is for it to find you,
and drink.

Appendix Australis

1. See Highfield, Taylor, Farrell, Dunk. The post-Federation asphyxiation with native animals in children's literature operates as a bypass to questions of personified Aboriginal presence, further clearing land for the inscription of national and environmental connections through cryptototemic relationships. By extension, we might consider the function of native animal guides as an attempt to naturalise their claim to the land as inheritors of its wisdom and recognition. Committing, then, to the premise: we must recognise the elisions and contradictions which desperately tremor at something beyond settler comprehension and containment as nothing more than the new trick of an old dog.

2. op. cit., smh: To appease the ongoing anxiety of displacement of the European body and psyche beyond the idyllic safety of the European pastoral. Pg 1919: To appease the ongoing anxiety of the precious white bub disappearing through the trees. Taylor (ibid.): To remind and resurface the repressed settler fear that there was nothing that could tame the wilderness, nothing that might make home of the unhomely.

3. Figure 18-99 depicts the settler/native binary, in which the safety of the child is predicated not simply on their return to the scene of the settler homestead, but their disavowal of uncivilised or transgressive behaviour.

4. See Pedley, Gibbs, see the cross-stitch marked $8.99 on the back wall of Vinnies, or purchase for $A230 through our Instagram boutique. Take sympathy for the many

beautiful and frolicsome creatures of their fair land, whose extinction – through ruthless destruction – is surely being accomplished. Please be kind to all bush creatures and don't pull flowers up by the roots.

5. sic: haunt, not hunt.

6. et seq. these texts exemplify models of mutually determined belonging for both settler humans and Indigenous animals in their rejection of the untameable presence of Aboriginal bodies and practices in the bush. cf. Kangaroo repudiating her human relations for their perceived savagery in favour of the daughter of that which desires industrially to slaughter her with the little white bubs casting from the bush the atavistically charged Banksia Men with their skinny black legs and wide black mouths.

7. passim: The over-determination of these tropes and compulsions to exorcise the extant sensation of a profound alienation from the landscape, the tyranny of distance from European pastoral and folkloric traditions, the forgetting that the Other might one day read what was wrote.

8. sic: ghost gums don't grow on the Hawkesbury.

9. For a more detailed analysis take the bus up Palmyra and swing it down towards Wilmott. Knock three times at the first house on the corner and tell them I sent you.

10. Blinky, Nutsy, et al. Referenced every afternoon at 4.

11. Further: Such attempts to recall or ironise these conventions in the last two decades of conceptual poetics must be read alongside, and not in resistance to, recent commercial recuperation of such aesthetics. See Figure 12: *Banksia Tattoo, Brunswick.*

12. ante. ante. ante.

13. Stolen from the Woiwurrung, meaning 'to join' or 'annex'. Henceforth shall be removed from text for violation of intellectual property and basic principles.

14. et seq. although one strategy seems to suggest a more ethically considerate response, Hodge and Mishra argue that each does their own form of violence – the former erasing Aboriginal people from literature, while the latter from history, into the mythic void of the Dream Time.

15. cf. resin brooch or hand-dyed linen smock.

16. Otherwise: Sacrifice the goanna, the blacksnake, bury your workmates tanned to leather by a hostile sun, mumble a few words in their honour at twilight. Raise resilient children, lie half awake at night as possum claws rake the corrugated iron, build, dwell, expand, maybe eventually belong. But you won't, not really – the spectre of what you're trying to conceal is written in the metrics of your bush ballad, etched everywhere in the wide dark watching the solitary homestead, waiting for the final breath that puffs out the last candle when you've muttered that prayer to the wrong hemisphere's god.

17. trans.: fuck off back to your own country, sic.

18. Further: The suggestion of an environmentally and culturally situated movement against globalism towards a pre-national and postcolonial identity can be countered by observing the form's compulsive translation back to Western aesthetic terms, suggesting this movement does little more than further operationalise Aboriginal bodies and culture as settler psychosis. See Figure 6: *Tea Towel, Your Mum's House.*

19. See *Aborigines Protection Act 1909* (New South Wales), which particularly focused on the removal of Aboriginal children into training institutions or unpaid labour.

20. According to: Amethyst and her cousin Aaron, the old lady nicked that one from a black woman who cleaned her house down on the coast.

21. Contact stockists for full product selection, including: Rompers, Bandanas and Other Hair Accessories, Socks, Leggings, Quilting Fabric, Wall Decals, Gardening Tools, Stationery and Calligraphy, Kitchen (including cups, saucers, dining sets, cutlery, coasters etc.), Reusable Cups (plastic, silicone, terracotta, glass), Personalised Sticker and Iron-On Labels, Decorative Wall Hoops, Swimwear, Hats and Caps, Window Displays, Brooches and Other Jewellery, Totes and Bags, Bedspreads and Cushion Covers, Bloomers and Nappy Covers, Wall Hangings and Prints, Plushies, Sandshoes, Christmas Ornaments, Aprons, Commemorative Coins, Lighting Displays, School Holiday Craft Projects (with free PDF download), Polymer Stamps, Keyrings, Kakadu Plum and Marshmallow Organic Baby Skincare, Wooden Toys, Wash Bags, Food Storage, Play Mats, Adult Fashion, Costumes, Face Masks.

22. Full line, from Paterson: *'Tis strange that in a land so strong / So strong and bold in mighty youth / We have no poet's voice of truth.*

23. Note: no permissions were granted by community for this usage.

24. trans.: The notion that there is art in acknowledging genocide, the suggestion we are readymades for your songs.

25. In response to Eipper's depiction of Snugglepot and Cuddlepie as a lesbian heterotopia.

26. From personal correspondence, Twitter: 'bitch who the fuck gave you the audacity'.

27. In repudiation of Highfield's contention that *The Crocodile Hunter* represents a possibility of Australian Indigenous anticolonial culture.

28. From Tuck, Yang: decolonisation is not a metaphor. From Tuck, Ree: yes, I am telling you a story, but you may be reading another one.

29. quod vide, she doesn't speak for that river.

30. In reference to Poetry Reading, Sydney, 2018: your body is not the ghost gum, your fingers not sea reeds, your eyes not shining like the brushtail curled against the tree – your body is invasive and these are not your relations to claim.

31. Reference belonging to Matthews, Marne, Barker, Simms, Nipps: do not disturb the journey, do not pass without greeting, do not forget who made this place.

32. McCann: Here, modernity demands human sacrifice. The spectre will be romantic, noble – a metropolis built on bones.

33. Wybalenna, good health, go to hell.

34. Dear Sir or Madam No I Cannot Advise on Your:
    a. Poem/Play/Novel/Monograph
    b. Tattoo
    c. Family story
    d. Plans to most wokefully distribute a fraction of your inheritance from your _____ ancestors:
        i. Slave-owning
        ii. Mine-owning
        iii. Land-owning

35. The term 'necropastoral' has been borrowed by ecopoetics before completion of service it owes to the people who were buried in the land, not those who stole it.

36. D, I am reckoning with my willingness to let the earth take back its generosity.
37. sic: not a fucking ghost gum, ibid.
38. Re: who told you you could speak for my totem?
39. In demonstration of: the necessity of entertainment for the pretty white children which erases the ugly black children so they might forever know their place is nowhere. In demonstration of: nostalgia as a compulsive return to a site of longing, and trauma as a condition of inheritance.
40. Don't say Reconciliation Action Plan, say fuck the police.
41. Take me back to ante. ante. ante. so I might rest in the soil and never have to read a poem again.
42. In reference to original question: does the land actually want you?
43. I would like to respect honour and remember the ancestors who spilt white blood for this place.

Unreckoning

Sis, I have a ghost story:

A river flows fat with bream and cod and perch. Here where the soil has parted for the belly of creators, the stones in shape of the foot of god, the river ripples songs for their journeys through the land. Black bodies splash shards of golden light, there is enough and enough and enough. I promise where we stand now, sis, on the dusty banks of the basin where a dry-dead rivergum slouches brittle into the spelching mud is only memory for the water that gathers and makes green the living.

Under and over the silence and clunky chains of the colonising tongue, there is speaking in the rustle of leaf and call of bird. These are the words the land knows, for it made them in the cradles of country, in the salt and sand of sound. Songs carry through track and tract, lines are traced so the living know where to dance. I swear nothing of the immemorial slumbers, sis. This is the voice I use to call you, and the one you use to answer.

I know there are other everywhens and not far from ours, sis, the sun burns behind mountain to light campfires in the sky. A child returns from the day to waiting arms. There is water and language and loving in all the rites of home. She knows her name, and her mother's name, and her grandmother's name, and the names of ancestor and relation and creation, and the names of those who will come. She knows the earth that knows her. She is home and she will never be made to leave.

Sis, I'm haunted in and out of dreaming. I don't know if we're the nightmares.

FOR POWER FOR PRAYER
FOR PROMISE FOR PEACE

IN THE ABSENCE OF POWER, SAY WE WILL NOT
FORGET //
IN THE THOUGHTS AND PRAYERS, SAY WE WILL
NOT SETTLE FOR SILENCE //
TO THOSE WHO ARE COMING, WE PROMISE WE
WILL NOT LEAVE //
IF THERE WILL BE NO JUSTICE, WE WILL NOT
PERMIT PEACE //

the bloodied face of history is black,
is bruise spilling from a mouth
that won't swallow its own tongue
// the face of history is a
death mask smothered against beautiful black
// is a bullet to the back is a body to the wall
// is holy   like howling to forever
that the sky has another star to burn

// the prayer for peace says second to
send grief to the soil //
but first to take it back
// says there are some things
too hallowed for forgetting //
too much of history to forgive

// the fury the gun the cell the throat
nothing more holy // nothing
more left to lose no lord no glory only
the blood back to the earth // only
mothers weeping to the street only
    //   //   //   //

THE POEM SAYS, SPEAK THE AFTERMATH OF
HISTORY //
THE WALL SAYS, FUCK THE POLICE //
THE CRY ON THE STREET SAYS, SAY THEIR NAMES:
    AGAINST EVERY CEREMONY WE TRACE TO
    JOURNEY THEM HOME, SAY THE WORD
    THAT WILL BIND THEM HERE UNTIL WE
    MIGHT LET THEM LEAVE WITH JUSTICE.
IF YOU SAY FORGIVENESS, LET IT BE WITHOUT A
KNEE TO A NECK //

See You Tonight

We're losing light now, but never rhythm,
     spilling between house and yard.
Mum's got her feet up, and I'm making that
curry you all like. Dad's in the shed but he'll
hear if we call. The sky burns vermilion behind
the gum stretching from our trickle of South
Creek, a corella keening in its hollow. Every night
is this one, the same sun browning our shared
limbs on its way to sink over city that's too far for
us to care. Take long walks, play with the dogs,
tell me how was work after I scream at you for
stealing my shoes again. Did you see that big roo
coming in? Heat rising from the scrub. Go look
at Mum's new quilt, she used the red blossom print
you liked. At the table, tell the one about finding
the owl in the van, remember those white gums across
from the old house. We always said we'd swim the
dam one day. You play bunyip, I'll be dropbear.
Your arm still hurts some nights from my bike,
so do my dreams. If all we get from history
is each other, isn't that plenty? I hope this living
is long enough for me to bathe your children, to
brush their hair. I'm saving them that book of
bush songs, those gumnut onesies. Cicadas wail
to the moon watching us above silhouettes.
Didn't she ever tell you that one? It's all good,
     I will, I will, I will.

THE LAST BUSH BALLAD

Up and out and over the gum gully the bubs and babes are all about imagining remembering on a melancholic waltz through the ruins of den and drey and paragon cafe. With each step each they pluck a piece of debris for their dilly bags to rattle about with gumnut coin and sugarbush comb and all else packed for the great roving through the dried and drowned burgs. Passing per shanty up the hill they call callooh callay to the bush and highway men making honest livings of honest pub verandahs, to the humpies down the nullah they sneer at the hunters for their violence to them and other bush creatures, and to the ghost gums manifest on the horizon they pay their proper ancestral tributes and prayers. The littles are all apoke and ajeer in performing to each other these tree bandit dialectics, adive and asquat in the scrub the native bears screaming to the native dogs COME OUT OR I'LL EAT YOU TO DEATH! Soon their dillys are dragging like tails in the red dirt so they must all make their public looting and private leering marsupial, these and other acts are their larrikin work and they promise important apocalyptic doings to the nuclear that will be both dechemical and decolonial.

Leaving the woodchipped Greenpatch the court remurmurs the wondrous song the Gumnut Editors have been backward scribbling until time immaterial on every barked signpost of White City's commuter belt, its tones what whisper only to those who know the Bush and love it well. It is the strain that steams from the billy, the ditty that dangles from the swagman's coolibah. Even the fringes and eccentrics of the movement know the most famous of the pronouncement – The Way Is Won! The Way Is Won! There is better country further out and the mountains shall watch us march by! Weaving out and about the creeks and gullies they remind themselves in the national rings and chimes – we shall reach the sea and drown the Banksia Men if we survive the Bunyip! We shall reach the sea and drown the Bunyip if we escape the Dropbear! For since the haunting of the axe to strike the gum what built the boats to bear the breed they have always known the breath it was that woke the silence they were first not to hear: that this land had no poets but it had thirst and rage and dreaming.

The dillys pulling down the pouches they now collect their rust findings in swags and coolamons. The bittier bubs take cockroach steeds and the bigger roo cabs, most making mode of leather boots and calcified bones and the very hardest of yakker. As the wideness dusks to dark the ghost gum globes are all aflicker in guidance as the troop go marching on, yes indeed in view of the mountains who have thrown back in echo COME OUT OR I'LL EAT YOU TO DEATH! The band, not remembering their own proclamations, are all aterror in fear of Banksia or Bunyip or Dropbear cry, and begin a great rushing forth to the waters they spy ashine the southern horizon. Each and every artefact comes tipping and tumbling out about their bounding bodies, acrash and asmash on the shuddering surface.

The Way Is Won! The Way Is Won! We have found the better country further out! the many creatures rejoice in advancement of the shore. *We have reached the sea to drown*

the Banksia Men, we have survived the Bunyip, we have
escaped the Dropbear! We have done our doings and our work!

In the great jangle and tangle amidst the great drowning
under tide and tithing they did not notice the mountain's
mimesis, which in the voice of all the vengeful ancestors
was heard to be lyred and said: I told you this was a thirst
so great it could carve rivers. I told you I was prepared to
swallow.

NOTES

Several poems and essays throughout this collection riff off and respond to popular tropes, icons and texts of Australian national culture. Some lines directly reference writers such as Kenneth Slessor, D.H. Lawrence, May Gibbs, Ethel Pedley and Banjo Paterson. Others more abstractly evoke the iconography of particular literary and cultural movements or ideas. A fuller account of the paraphrased scholarly references mentioned in 'Playing in the Pastoral' and 'Appendix Australis' can be read in the companion essay to this book, 'Snugglepot and Cuddlepie in the Ghost Gum', published by *Sydney Review of Books* (February 2019). Any responses to this intertextuality, and the tone in which it is presented, should be read with the understanding that the material and political reality of the colonial past which Indigenous peoples inherit is also a literary one. Our resistance, therefore, must also be literary.

'GATHER' is written in response to Jeanine Leane's poetic writing on gathering and gatherers.

'Index Australis' is written as a dialogue and response to Soda Jerk's 2018 film *Terror Nullius*, and also features references to the songs of Nick Cave and the Bad Seeds.

In 'Playing in the Pastoral', the term *'artifactualitied'* in this usage was developed by Michael R. Griffiths, described in his book *The Distribution of Settlement: Appropriation and Refusal in Australian Literature and Culture* (UWA Publishing, 2018). The section 'and it was dreamt … gods and men left behind', as well as the later line 'the space and sun and unworn-out air', paraphrase several lines from D.H. Lawrence's novel *Kangaroo* (Martin Secker, 1923). The lines 'For: the well-meant impetuosity of a young colony' and 'For: the vacant office in the *Bulletin* for some mythological creature to make itself useful' are both references to remarks pertaining to the history of Australian national iconography in Vane Lindesay's *Aussie-Osities* (Greenhouse Publications, 1988). The line 'For: the settler move to innocence' refers to a concept described by Eve Tuck and K. Wayne Yang by which settler colonies seek to legitimate their destruction of Indigenous lifeworlds in their seminal essay, 'Decolonization is not a metaphor', published in *Decolonization: Indigeneity, Education & Society*, vol. 1, no. 1, 2012, pp. 1–40.

'The Last Endeavour', like its companion poem 'THE LAST BUSH BALLAD', contains a series of references derived from a great range of Australian literature. Source materials include the publications and journals of Banjo Paterson, D.H. Lawrence, Samuel Coleridge, Watkin Tench and Thomas Mitchell. The lines 'man could be noble like this' and 'Too good, too good, this eloquent offering of birdcage to gulls' are variations on lines from Kenneth Slessor's 1931 poem 'Five Visions of Captain Cook'.

'The Trope Speaks' compiles sections of my own academic writing on Australian national culture with paraphrased or inverted found texts from childhood books, including Dorothy Wall's *Blinky Bill and Nutsy: Two Little Australians* (Angus & Robertson, 1937) and Will Douglas's *The Bush Alphabet* (Hale & Iremonger, 1986). The lines 'The trope contracts, its planks creak, but its grandfather built it to last and it knows its roofs and verandahs will give just enough to survive unscathed' paraphrases Les Murray's 1966 poem 'Evening Alone at Bunyah'.

'Guarded by Birds' was originally published by *Overland* as the winner of the Judith Wright Poetry Prize in 2018. The line 'too goodtoo good / this eloquent offering / of birdcage to gulls' is a variation on a line from Kenneth Slessor's 1931 poem 'Five Visions of Captain Cook'.

'Mrs Kookaburra Addresses the Natives' uses found text material from May Gibbs's Snugglepot and Cuddlepie books.

The line *all the little devils are proud of hell'* in 'In Fright' is from the 1971 film *Wake in Fright*, directed by Ted Kotcheff. The line 'the virus missed me to strike a child starving someplace / closer than I want to know' is a reference to Donte Collins's 2016 poem 'What the Dead Know by Heart'. The line 'we haven't had a storm this bad since you took out that tender ship of mine' is a quotation from the 'Two Cathedrals' episode of Aaron Sorkin's 1999–2006 show *The West Wing*.

'Fern Up Your Own Gully' makes reference to the 1992 animated film *FernGully: The Last Rainforest*, directed by Bill Kroyer, and related promotional material.

'FOMO' makes reference to remarks made in archival materials pertaining to the 1879 destruction of Sydney's Garden Palace, and artist Jonathan Jones's 2016 installation *barrangal dyara (skin and bones)*.

In 'THE LAST BUSH BALLAD', placenames, such as Greenpatch and White City, are from the stories of Blinky Bill and Snugglepot and Cuddlepie, respectively. The line 'The Way Is Won' is a refrain from Banjo Paterson's poem 'Song of the Future', published in the *Bulletin* in 1889.

ACKNOWLEDGEMENTS

I would like to acknowledge and pay my respects to the many countries from which this book was written. I mark with honour and reverence the lands of the Dharug, Wangal, Gadigal, Tharawal, Woi Wurrung, Wurundjeri, Turrbal, Yugambeh, Bundjalung, Yuin, Darkinjung, Yorta Yorta, Wiradjuri, Gamilaraay, Gomeroi and Worimi, and also to the original custodians of Ireland, Wales and England. I thank the creators, ancestors, traditional owners and custodians of these lands for the ongoing care and generosity.

The cultural knowledge discussed in this book has been informed by many generations of Aboriginal Elders. I would particularly like to acknowledge and extend my reverence to Aunty Gloria Matthews, Uncle Wes Marne, Uncle Greg Simms and Aunty Charlotte Nipps. I would also like to thank some of the incredible Aboriginal women who have kept me honest in my growth: Lorna Munro and her mother, Aunty Jenny Munro, for always demonstrating true leadership and accountability. Amethyst Downing for the greatest generosities of spirit imaginable. Sheelagh Daniels-Mayes for supporting me both personally and professionally to keep me enrolled at uni, no matter how many times I turned up to a supervision meeting in tears. Jeanine Leane for always demanding what's right, and always pushing for the best outcomes in our literary landscape. Alison Whittaker for being literally the kindest person I've ever met. Melissa Lucashenko for always being there to extend care and encouragement. Alexis Wright for inspiration and leadership. Aunty Kerry Reed-Gilbert for the legacy she built. Natalie Harkin for the power and sensitivity so willingly shared throughout our community. I would like to thank and honour Ellen van Neerven for their years of support and wisdom, and for the tenderness and intellectual strength they brought to this manuscript.

This book means nothing without my family – Mum and Dad, and my beautiful siblings, James, Amelia, Magdalen, Verity and Grace. I adore all of you, and am so grateful for your gifts. My deepest gratitude goes to Jonathan Dunk for this and everything else: you are truly the most remarkable person I've ever met, and I'm so lucky to know you. Love also to Silvia, Caitlin, Kate, Annie, David, Alice, and especially big love to Melody Paloma for encouraging this manuscript from the start. Thanks to Peter Minter for all the years of patience – I promise I'll graduate someday. Thank you to Tony Birch for your mentorship and feedback on my messy drafts, and also to Aviva Tuffield at UQP for bringing this project to a fruition that I could not fully envision myself. I'd also love to thank Jenna Lee for her gorgeous artwork and for the care with which she approached my ideas.

This book was written with the support of the *Overland* Nakata Brophy Young Indigenous Writers residency at Trinity College, the University of Melbourne; The Wheeler Centre's Next Chapter Fellowship and its sponsors, the Aesop Foundation; the Varuna Writers' House; Writers Victoria's Neilma Sidney Literary Travel Fund; and Sweatshop Western Sydney. I also wish to recognise the Jindaola project at the University of Wollongong, the Malcolm Robertson Foundation's support for the *Overland* Judith Wright Poetry Prize, and the First Nations Australia Writers Network.

Several poems in this collection have been previously

published or commissioned. 'The Ghost Gum Sequence', 'Playing in the Pastoral', 'To the Poets', 'To the Parents' and 'THE LAST BUSH BALLAD' appeared in an essay for *Sydney Review of Books* as part of their *New Nature Archives*. 'Learning Bundjalung on Tharawal', 'Dropbear Poetics' and 'Guarded by Birds' were published by *Overland Literary Journal*. 'Pyro', 'Mrs Kookaburra Addresses the Natives', 'FOMO' and 'FOR POWER FOR PRAYER FOR PROMISE FOR PEACE' were published by *Australian Poetry*. 'Malay' first appeared in *The Big Black Thing: Chapter 2*, published by Sweatshop in 2018. 'decolonial poetics (avant gubba)' and 'Wangal Morning' were published by *Cordite Poetry Review*. 'Home, After the Fire' was published by *Peril*. 'Bahloo' and 'K1: Yellomundee' were published by the Red Room Poetry Company. 'Fern Up Your Own Gully' was published by *The Lifted Brow*. 'Unreckoning' was published in *The Saturday Paper*. 'Secret River' was commissioned by Daniel Browning on behalf of *Urban Theatre Projects*. 'Stutter' was commissioned by the National Gallery of Australia for their exhibition *The Body Electric*. An earlier version of 'With Hidden Noise' was commissioned in collaboration with the Sydney Writers' Festival, the Art Gallery of New South Wales, Red Room Poetry Company and the Philadelphia Museum of Art.

Many lives and stories have been erased, exploited or violated in the short but haunted history of Australian literature. This book cannot redress the inequity this culture is built upon, but it is important to emphasise that it was written from a place of remembrance and honour for those forgotten or misused.